Cleveland Bays
"History and Future"
Horses For Kids

I0440780

Nature Books for Kids
By
K. Bennett

JD-Biz Publishing

All Rights Reserved.

No part of this publication may be reproduced in any form or by any means, including scanning, photocopying, or otherwise without prior written permission from JD-Biz Corp

Copyright © 2015. All Images Licensed by Fotolia and 123RF.

Read More Amazing Animal Books

Purchase at Amazon.com

Cleveland Bays

Table of Contents

Introduction

Author Bio

Introduction

"Somewhere, something incredible is waiting to be known."
– Carl Sagan

***

Cleveland Bay: Cleveland Bay horses are very special. Do you know why? Because they are the oldest breed of horses native to England!

Where do they come from?

These horses came from the Cleveland area of North Yorkshire in England. This is why they are called Cleveland Bays. But this is not the only reason for their name. What color are they? Can you guess? Do you remember what a Bay is?

Bay horses

Bay horses have a special coat color. Look at the pictures closely. What color do you think it is? Brown, dark red, dark brown or a mix of these colors? Ready? Drumroll please….The color is ***reddish brown!***

Now look at the legs. They are darker than the rest of the body. So these beautiful horses are reddish brown with a black mane, legs and tail.

Even the tips of the ears are black! This coloring is called "***black points***." This color is what makes the horse, and if it doesn't have these color characteristics, it cannot be a Cleveland Bay!

Note: Sometimes, a Bay will have white markings. For example, some of them have a small, white star on their forehead but the color is still Bay. Sometimes Cleveland Bays come in a Chestnut color, but this is rare to find.

So what do you think about the Bay's color? Do you like it?

A Chapman horse

These beautiful horses have an old heritage. Before they were known as Cleveland Bays, they were called "Chapman horses." Do you know why? They got this name from travelling salesmen or merchants who used Cleveland Bays to carry their goods.

What makes this horse special?

Cleveland Bays have a very interesting history and we will talk about that more in chapter 1. But did you know Cleveland Bays are the only non-draught or ***non-draft*** horses developed in the UK? What does that mean? Do you remember what a draft horse is?

A draft horse.

This is a horse that "draws" or "hauls" something. It is also called a work horse or heavy horse, because it works hard and pulls heavy loads. However, these types of horses are usually strong, gentle, easy to work with and very patient.

An Amazing Horse

Cleveland Bays are really amazing and smart! It's strength, versatility, stamina and personality is also one of a kind! With their beautiful coat, and rich ancestry, Cleveland Bays are lots of fun to learn about. I hope you take a moment to read a little more on this beautiful animal, and don't forget to share what you learn with others!

HOW TO DRAW A SIMPLE HORSE FOR KIDS:

Would you like to learn how to draw a horse? Wikihow.com has a simple, but neat tutorial. Here are the steps to get started:

1- First, ask your parent's or a guardian's permission to go online.

2- In your browser (Chrome, Internet explorer, Firefox, Torch) type: www.Wikihow.com

3- In the search box at the top of the page type: *Draw a simple horse*. Once the search is complete, you should see a title that reads: "**How to draw a simple horse: 11 steps with pictures**."

4 – Click on the link and follow the steps.

5- Have fun!

Cleveland Bays

Chapter 1

Hi, it's nice to meet you!

History: To understand where this beautiful horse came from, we have to go back in history to the time of Kings and Queens!

English Royalty

For over one hundred years, English Royalty has sponsored these amazing horses. They liked them so much that they used these beautiful horses to pull carriages and ride in processions. And this is still happening today. The Queen of England is a proud sponsor or Patron of this breed, and her Royal Mews continue to use this magnificent horse in ceremonial events.

Medieval times

It was not only Royalty that used these horses. The ancestors of Cleveland Bays came from churches and monasteries. And they were used to transport goods between these ancient places.

(Source: *Learn-about-horses.com*)

Development

Cleveland Bays were used as pack horses for many years. Remember how they helped the Salesmen to carry goods from one place to another? So they were not used in heavy draft work like other horses. But this doesn't mean they aren't strong. A horse needs a lot of energy and strength to carry goods around all day!

Cleveland Bays come from a strong mix of horses, but during the 17th and 18th century, these amazing horses were crossed with Andalusian and Arabian horses.

Then around the 19th century, the British Calvary saw something they really liked, and soon Cleveland Bays became "one of the most common draft and coach horses in Britain and the United States!"

(Source: *Britannica.com*)

What makes these horses so special?

Cleveland Bays are called "all-rounders." Does this sound strange to you? It simply means these horses are good for many different things like: Hunting, riding, pulling coaches, driving, working as a pack horse and doing agricultural work.

Sometime during the 19th century, Cleveland Bays were *crossbred* with Thoroughbred horses. Do you know what this word means?

The dictionary at Kids.Net.Au defines this word like this: "*(genetics) the act of mixing different species or varieties of animals or plants and thus to produce hybrids.*"

So they mixed the horses together to make a new horse! The new horse was the Yorkshire Coach Horse. This horse is pretty cool. There is no other horse like it in speed, style and power!

Sadly, when the mechanical age came around (This was the time of railroads, trains, agricultural machines and more), Cleveland Bays almost disappeared! And during World War I and World War II, it got much worse. By the 1960's, there were only five or six stallions that people knew about! Isn't that awful? But there is good news!

The people who admired this horse got together and decided to help them recover. And soon, Cleveland Bays started to grow in numbers again! (Sourse: *Imh.org*)

Today, this horse is used as "show jumpers" and hunters. It is also popular for driving and excellent for competition shows!

The wind feels good!

Cleveland Bays

FUN FACTS FOR KIDS: Measuring horses: What is **HANDS**?

This is a neat way to measure horses. The measurement refers to hands, literal hands! The symbol is usually HH (Hands high). So you would say 15hh, 16hh or 17hh. This means 15 hands, 16 hands and 17 hands. You might be wondering why people measure horses in hands?

Well, many years ago people did not have rulers or measuring sticks like we do today. So they used whatever they had…and they had hands. So horses are measured like this. You can do it too! How?

Think about it like this: One hand is 4 inches.

So if a horse is 15 hands multiply this by 4. (15 x 4) and you will get 60 inches. And if a horse is 16 hands multiply this number by 4. (16 x 4) and you will get 64 inches.

Cleveland Bays stand at 16 to 16.2 hands. Some stand at 17 hands. Can you do the math and find the inches?

Now that you know how to do it, you can measure other horses for yourself. Have fun!

Cleveland Bays

Awwwww this feels good!

Strengths: Cleveland Bays are strong horses with a heart of gold! But this is not all. They are also known as:

-Sensible
-Hardy
-Long lived
-Intelligent
-Calm
-Bold
-Honest
-Kind
-Tolerant
-Dignified

Which one of these traits do you have? Whichever one you pick means you have something in common with Cleveland Bays!

It is important to note Cleveland Bays have a strong personality. So if you don't treat them right, they can become hard to handle. This is not difficult to understand. **Remember:** All creatures want to be treated with love, kindness and respect. And if you don't treat them that way, they could lash out and hurt someone… even you. Just something to keep in mind!

One of the greatest strength of Cleveland Bays is their versatility. We have talked about this before, but do you really know what this word means?

Kids.net.Au says that when this word is used with people it means: "Having many skills."

You can think about the horse like this too! Cleveland Bays can do lots of different things that other horses may not be able to do in the same way. For example, they are great as:

-Pack and harness horses
-Carriage and driving horses
-Heavy weight hunters
-Exhibition horses
-Equine disciplines
-Police horses
-Event horses

That's a lot of different skills, right? And in each of them, these horses really stand out from the rest. Of course many people simply ride them for fun!

Weaknesses: Sadly, there are not many of these beautiful animals left. The *US American Livestock Breeds Conservancy* notes their status as critical. This means there are less than 2,000 around the world. And in one year there are less than 200 registered in the United States.

The Equus Survival Trust says there are only 100 to 300 breeding females registered around the world. So if you want to get a Cleveland Bay, it might be a little hard to find the "right" one!

However, if you are interested, equine magazines like "The Equine Journal" would be a great place to start. You could also check out the CBHSNA. They have names, addresses, numbers and emails of members with purebred horses.

CURIOUS FACT FOR KIDS:

During the mid-19th century, Show Jumping was just beginning and two horses were really good at it! Their names were Star and Fanny Drape.

Fanny Drape jumped over a 6 foot wall with a rider on her back and a 7.5 feet bar jumping in-hand. If you do not know what kind of jump this is (in-hand) ask your parent or a guardian to help you research what it means!

In 2006, another Cleveland Bay by the name of *Tregoyd Journeyman* participated in an event called: **Breyer' model horse festival**. Can you guess who the model for the new horse figure was?

(Source: *Wikipedia.org*)

Feels good to stretch my legs!

Training: Training a Cleveland Bay horse is in many ways like training other horse breeds. So let us detail the steps for training all horses to give you a better idea of how it's done.

Wikihow recommends the following steps:

1-***First of all, don't scare the horse***. That means you should not run up or sneak up on them suddenly. This is not a hard to understand. For example, do you like it when people run or sneak up on you suddenly? It may scare you when someone does that, right? Then a horse will feel the same way.

2-***Be gentle and talk gently to your horse***. There is no need to yell, shout or talk in a harsh tone to your horse. Again, this idea is not hard to understand. Do you like it when people talk to you gently? Or do you want them to shout and yell at you? Isn't it nicer to treat others kindly and don't you appreciate it when others do the same for you? Your horse will appreciate your kind manner too!

3-***Most horses love to be touched***. Show them your feelings through your hands. Stroke them on the head, massage their neck, hug them, brush them and communicate your affection through gentle fingers. Imagine how happy your horse will be!

4-***Try to spend as much time as you can with your horse***. In any friendship, regular visits are the key! No matter what you have to do, stop by and visit your horse just to remind them that you're there. They will be so happy to see you and the more you spend time with them, the stronger your bond will grow.

5- *A nice reward*. A tasty treat, rub or pat down, yummy food, grooming of whatever other treat you might have in mind, will be a great idea! Do this at the end of the day to let your horse know how much you enjoyed spending time with them.

Running is fun!

Chapter 2

Out for a walk with friends

Have you learned anything new about Cleveland Bays? Wonderful! But there is still a little bit more we can learn about them.

Because of their amazing abilities, Cleveland Bays are used in many disciplines, endurance competitions and riding skills. But guess what? They excel in dressage! That means that of all horses, they are really good at it!

Do you remember what dressage is?

Dressage training: Dressage training has been around for a very long time. The USDF (United States Dressage Federation) organization lists different levels for this type of skill.

There are five levels:

-Training level
-First level

-Second level
-Third level
-Fourth level

Before you begin this type of training, there are several things to do. *Wikihow.com* suggests the following steps.

1- Both you and your horse need to know each other very well! And you need to know if you can trust each other. So a close relationship is very important before any training can begin!

2- You have to start to work on the way your horse walks or trots. This is referred to as a **gait**. It is very important for your horse to walk in the right way.

3- **Transitions:** This is when you want your horse to change from one movement to another. It is important that this step is done in a smooth manner. It should be just like putting one footstep in front of the other without tripping over your feet!

4- Your position in the saddle should look comfortable and balanced! And your heels should be down at all times.

5 – Practice makes perfect. To get good at any skill, you need to do it over and over again. Practicing with your horse is a great way to get good at riding him!

Of course there are many other steps to dressage that is very important. But these are some of the basic ideas. If you want to learn more, ask your parent or a guardian to help you research!

Cleveland Bays are also great at ***Show Jumping***. Do you know what type of sport this is?

Wild and Free!

Show Jumping: You may already know that show jumping has to do with… jumping! But how does it work?

Well, the horse has to navigate or make its way across different types of obstacles or barriers. This happens inside a stadium or ring designed for these types of shows. During these events the horse is tested in different ways. For example, your horse will be tested for:

-Strength
-Stamina
-Speed and
-Flexibility…

And these skills are all very important. But wait…there's more! The horse also has to show its relationship with the rider. In other words, horse and rider should ride as one! So if you participated in this type of event, you and your horse should have a very, very good relationship. And more importantly, you need to be close friends!

Cleveland Bays

Why is this important? Guess who loses points if your horse makes a mistake? Yes! Both of you lose points, not just your horse. And if your horse decides not to make enough jumps, both of you will be disqualified. Ouch! Do you see why being friends with your horse is so important?

CURIOUS FACT FOR KIDS:

The Grand Prix is a show jumping event where the best horses compete. Horses like Cleveland Bays. The obstacles are complex, which means they are hard to finish! And the obstacles are intimidating, which means your horse may not like to do it!

Obstacles include hedges or ditches, which are high and long, so both you and your horse will really have to **focus** before you take the leap. The jumps are also placed at strange angles, which mean you have to **think** before you make the jump. Does this sound hard to do?

How good does your horse have to be? In the first place, your horse needs to be *quick* on its feet. It also has to be *skilled* and *adaptable* in order to complete the jobs successfully. Sounds hard? I think so too!

Typically, a rider will walk the course before the event. This allows both horse and rider to get a feel for the layout before the event.

Think about it like this: If you have a really hard typing test to do, isn't it a great idea to PRACTICE before the test? The same applies to competitions. After all, practice makes perfect!

(Source: *wisegeek.com*)

This grass is really soft!

Chapter 3

Here are a few additional characteristics about Cleveland Bays you may like to know.

-Cleveland Bays have a wide body and their back should be strong. The legs should be strong too! They also have plenty of bones and weigh between 1,400 and 1,500 pounds.

-Eyes are large and should have a kind look. This means when you look into their eyes someone kind should be staring back!

-Ears are usually large and fine, with beautiful "black points."

-Their feet are very important! They should be "best and blue" in color. This means they should look a certain way.

-The horse should also move around freely and the knees and hocks should flex easily!

(Source: **Imh.org**)

 ** If you don't recognize some of the words, whip out your dictionary and look them up!

Will you like to be my friend?

Cleveland Bays

GENERAL HORSE TIPS FOR KIDS:

If you are able to get a horse like the Cleveland Bay, you will need to care for it. So here are some tips you can think about. These basic principles apply to most if not all horses. Are you ready?

-Your horse's diet is very important. Some horses have very hot blood and some have cooler blood. If your horse is hot blooded, they will need less protein in their diet. Cleveland Bays are warm bloods.

-Learn how to properly discipline your horse. **Remember:** These animals are very sensitive and Cleveland Bays can really be affected if the discipline is done in the wrong way. Let them know when they are getting out of control! This can be done with a shhhhh noise or a firm tone to let them know who the master is!

-If the horse's head is high it means your horse is not relaxed. They may be upset in some way. If their head if low they are relaxed. Try to get your horse to stay relaxed. This will help them feel good and both of you will enjoy the ride.

-Horses love to get your tender rubs and soft pats. Things like rubbing their ears, nose, eyes and mouth is great. And a massage is even better!

-If a horse is trained really well, he or she will invite YOU for a ride. You should be looking for the invitation! Then you will enjoy an awesome ride.

-Your horse can sense your moods and behavior. If you are confident your horse will be confident too!

-You should feed your horse from a bucket and not your hand. (This is the recommendation, but I feel it is better to feed them with your hand from time to time! It seems to generate more trust and respect, but that is just my humble opinion on the subject. What do you think?)

(Source: Frank Bell- *Horsewhisperer.com*)

Cleveland Bays

And more interesting facts:

-A horse can express its emotions in many different ways. It can use its face, eyes and ears to tell you how it feels!

-Horses are great at keeping watch. It is rare to see a herd with everyone snoozing at one time. There is usually one horse standing as a lookout, and his job is to warn the others if danger comes near!

- Avoid standing behind a horse. They have great vision, but there are a couple of blind spots. Can you guess what the back part of the horse is? Yes! It's a blind spot. If the horse gets angry or scared, guess what he might do if you stand directly behind him?

-Horses are great at listening! They can turn their ears in different ways to improve their hearing. If you whisper and say something bad about your horse, they just might hear you!

- Horses can help people get better when they have mental or health problems. This is called: *Equine Assisted Therapy*.

-Horses are the best sleepers on the planet. They can sleep lying down and standing up! Can you do that?

- Horses are herbivores. Do you know that this means? It means they eat plants or are plant eaters, if you like this term better.

(Source: *Onekind.org*)

Conclusion

Bonding together

In conclusion: Perhaps they best way to describe the Cleveland Bay is by the words of Sir J D Paul in a poem published by the Whitby Gazette (England) in 1879 when he said: ***"All things that live have parallel, save one: The Cleveland Bay Horse, he alone has none!"***.

Do you agree with him? Then make time to learn a bit more about these noble animals. And if you don't know where to look, ask your teacher, a parent or guardian to help you. They may have some great ideas too!

You may not know exactly what to research about this noble breed, but perhaps you can choose something you really like about it. It can be the tail, mane, ears, body, size, personality, history, etc. Then investigate a bit more about that particular subject.

If you are in school and participate in show and tell, use that as your subject. Or if you have to make a report for school on animal life, why not choose the Cleveland Bay? Many of your classmates may not even know what a Cleveland Bay is really like, so it would be nice to share what you find with others!

I hope this book has taught you just how wonderful nature is and how each creature can impact our life in amazing ways.

And remember: *"Educating the mind without educating the heart is no education at all."* - *Aristotle*

Author Bio

K. Bennett loves to write for both children and adults. Many different subjects are interesting to develop, but writing for children is special to her heart.

Her favorite pastimes include reading, traveling and discovering new things. Each of these activities helps to fuel her imagination and acts like a blank canvas waiting for more stories.

She is intrigued with fantasy elements like hidden worlds and faraway lands. Basically anything that gets her imagination soaring to new heights!

Her writing credits include children books online, short stories for online magazines, and two novellas listed at Amazon.com

Our books are available at

1. Amazon.com

2. Barnes and Noble

3. Itunes

4. Kobo

5. Smashwords

6. Google Play Books

Publisher

JD-Biz Corp

P O Box 374

Mendon, Utah 84325

http://www.jd-biz.com/

Read more books from John Davidson

Amazon.com Author Link

Cleveland Bays

Cleveland Bays

www.ingramcontent.com/pod-product-compliance
Lightning Source LLC
Chambersburg PA
CBHW050922290526
45792CB00002B/859